I0465078

Totally Radical SPORTS Coloring Book

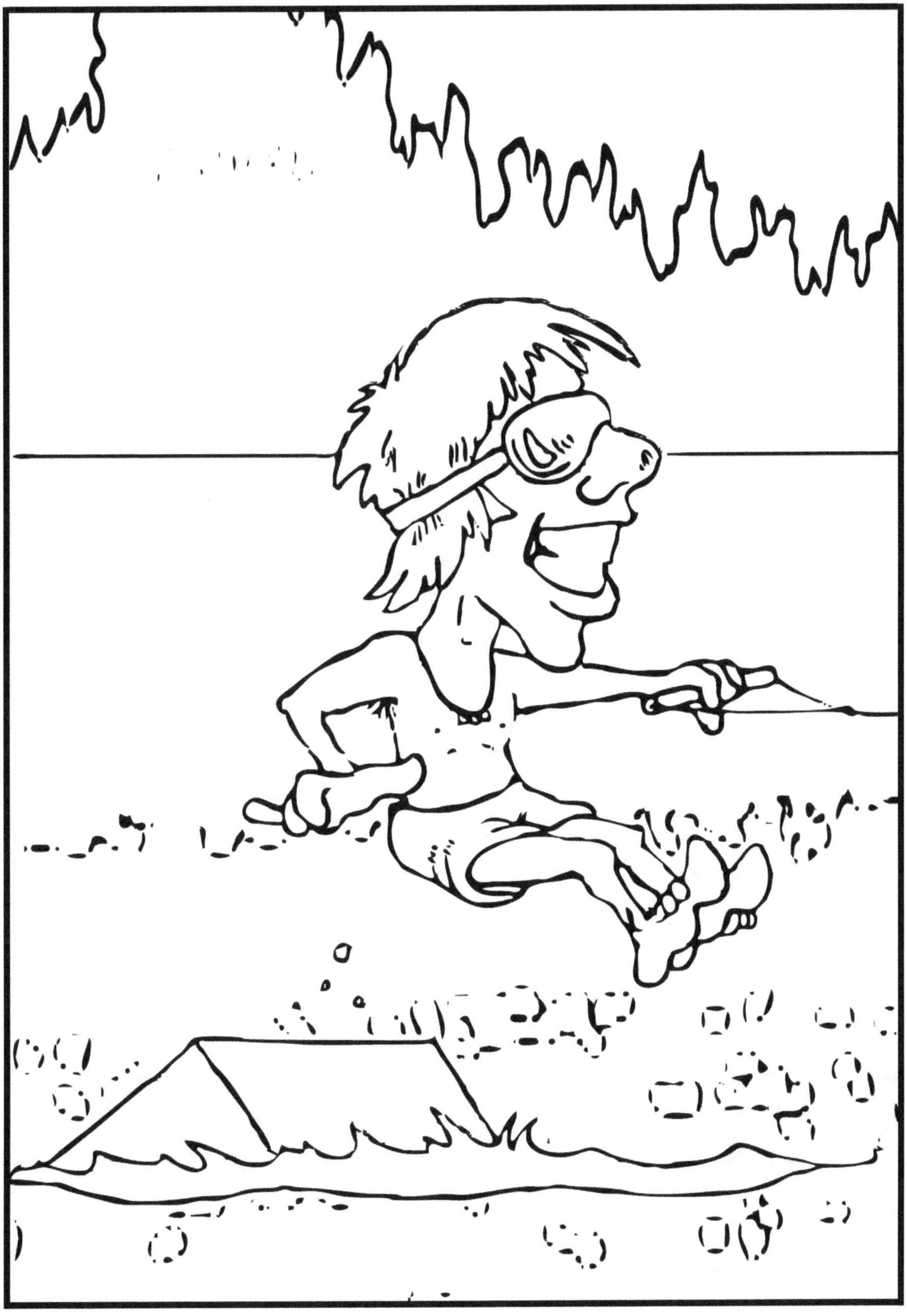

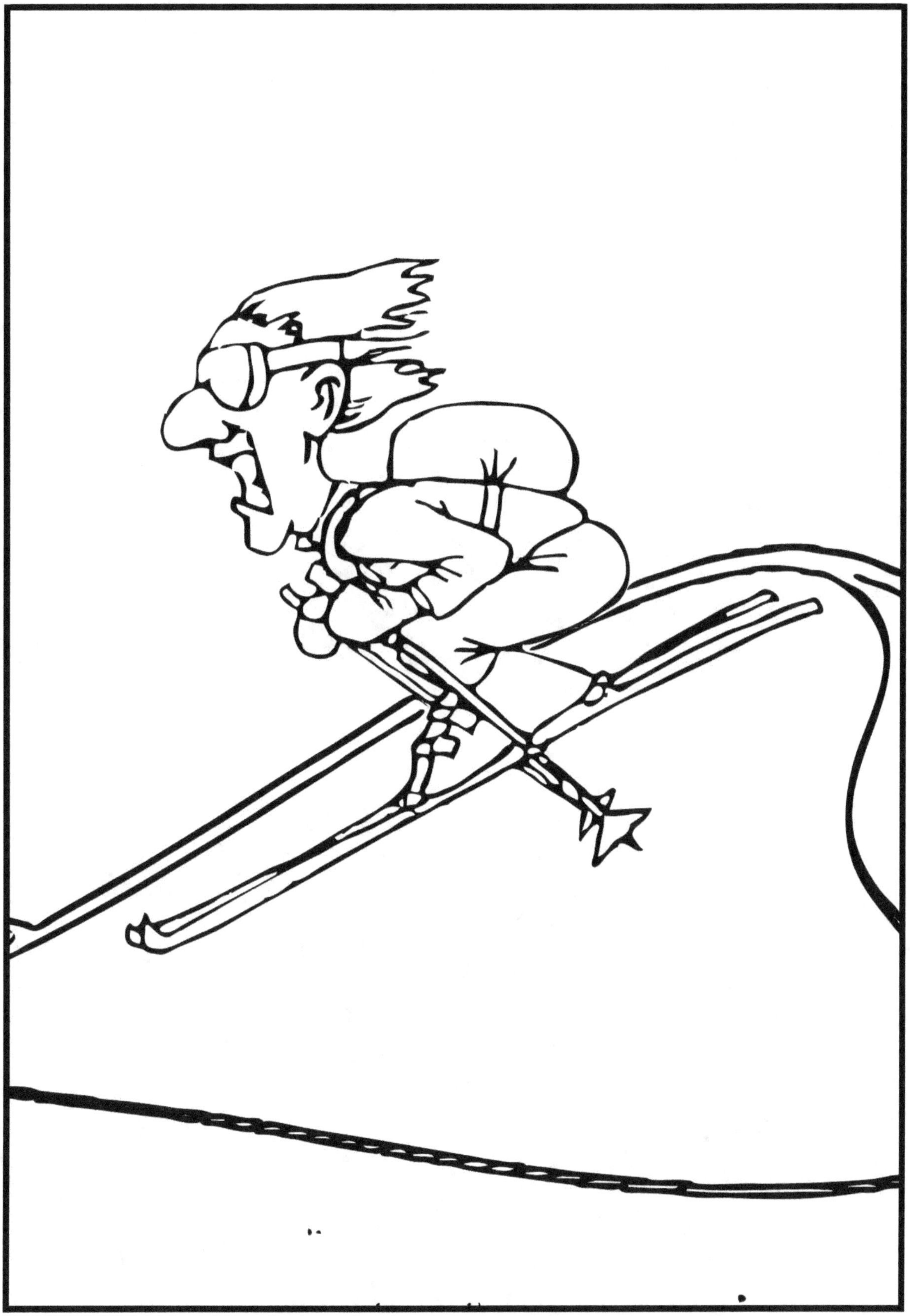

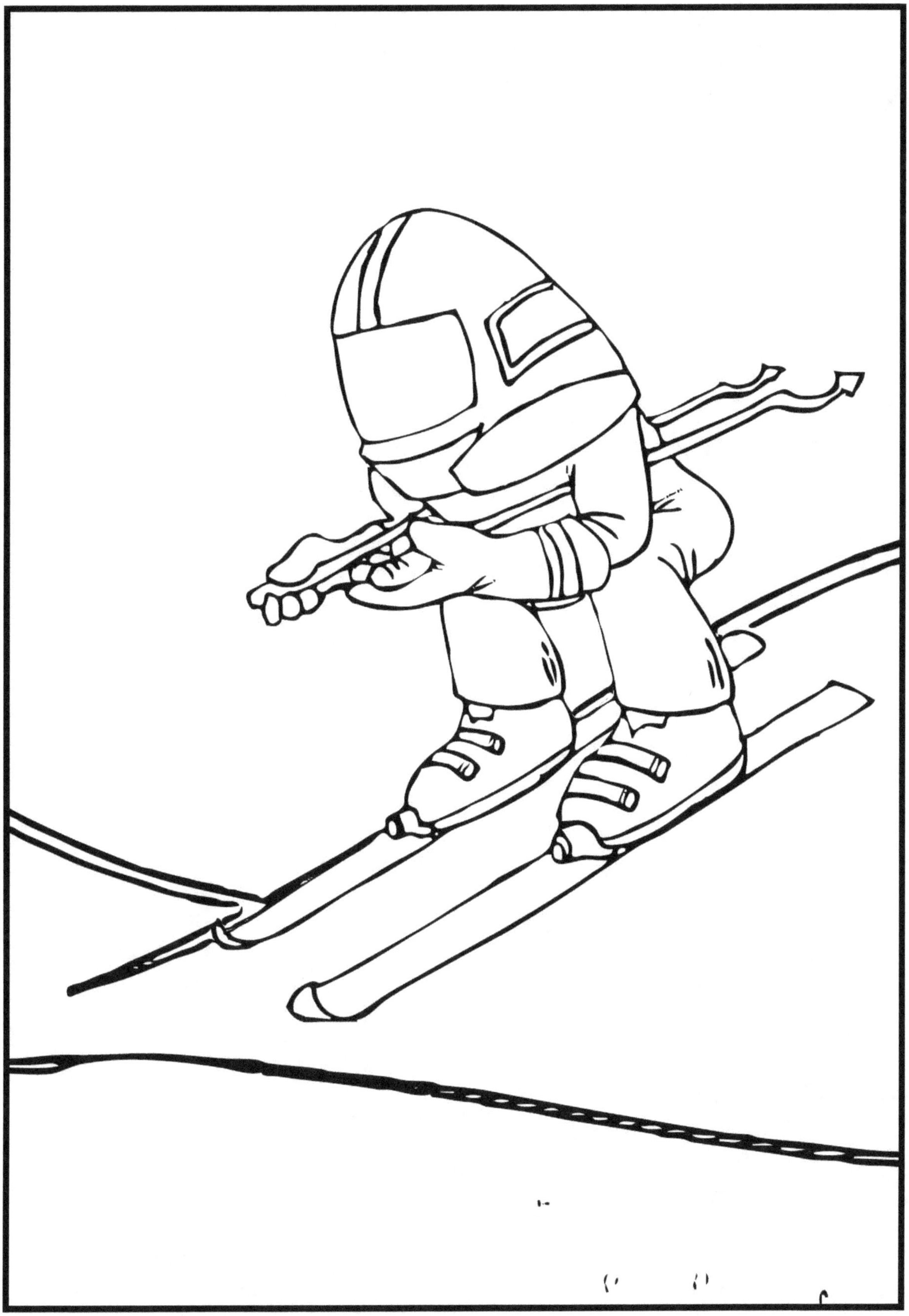

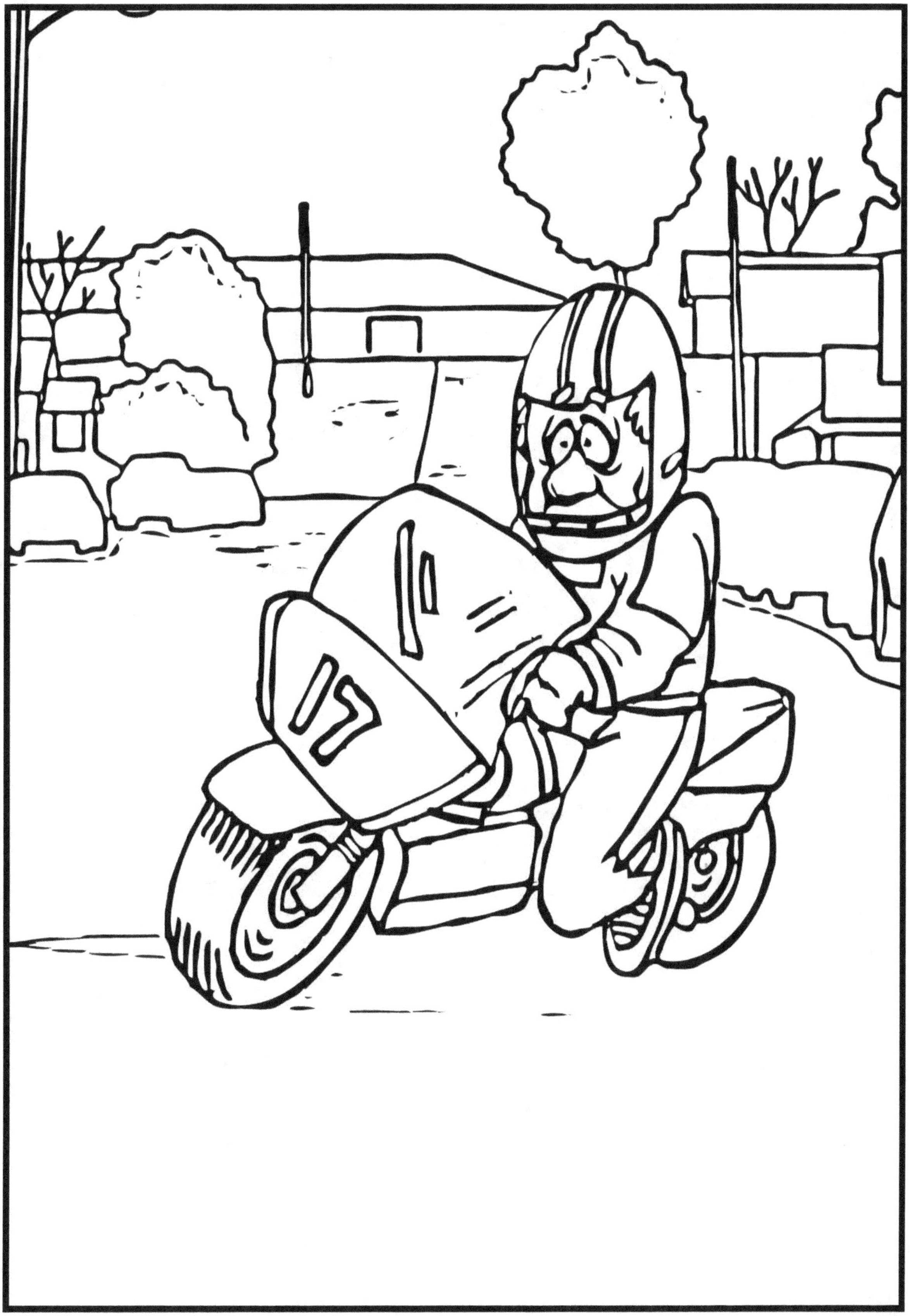
17

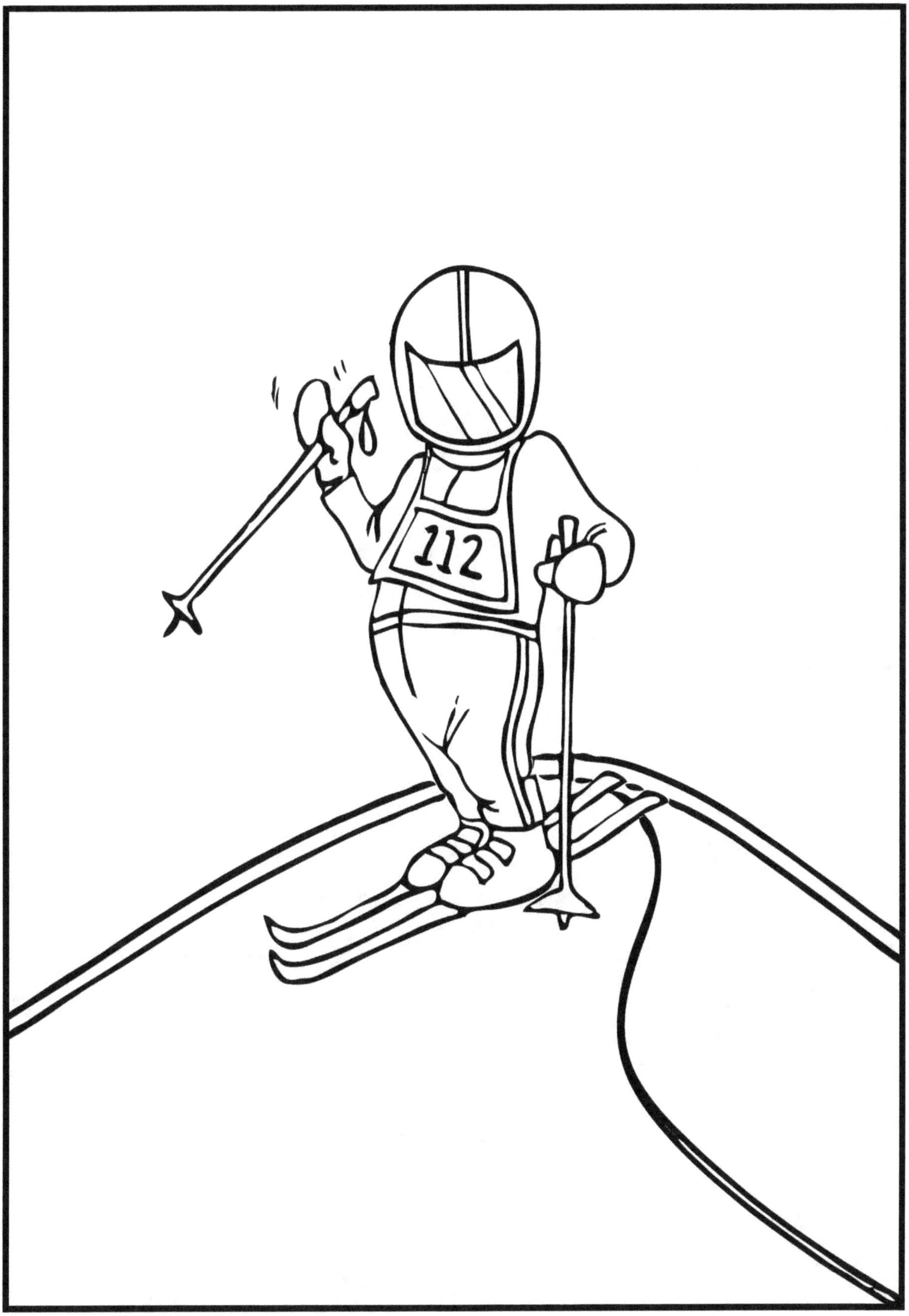
112

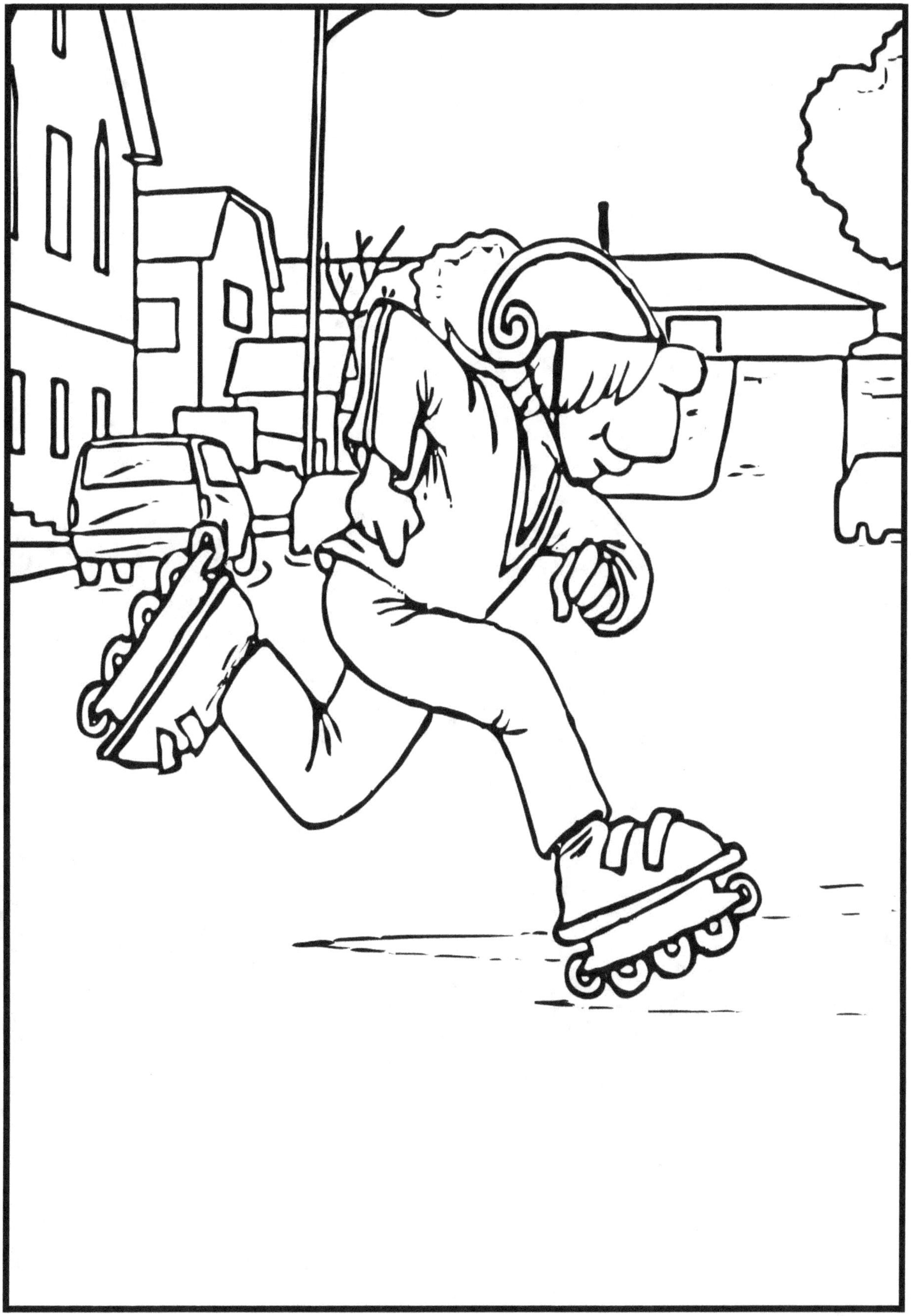

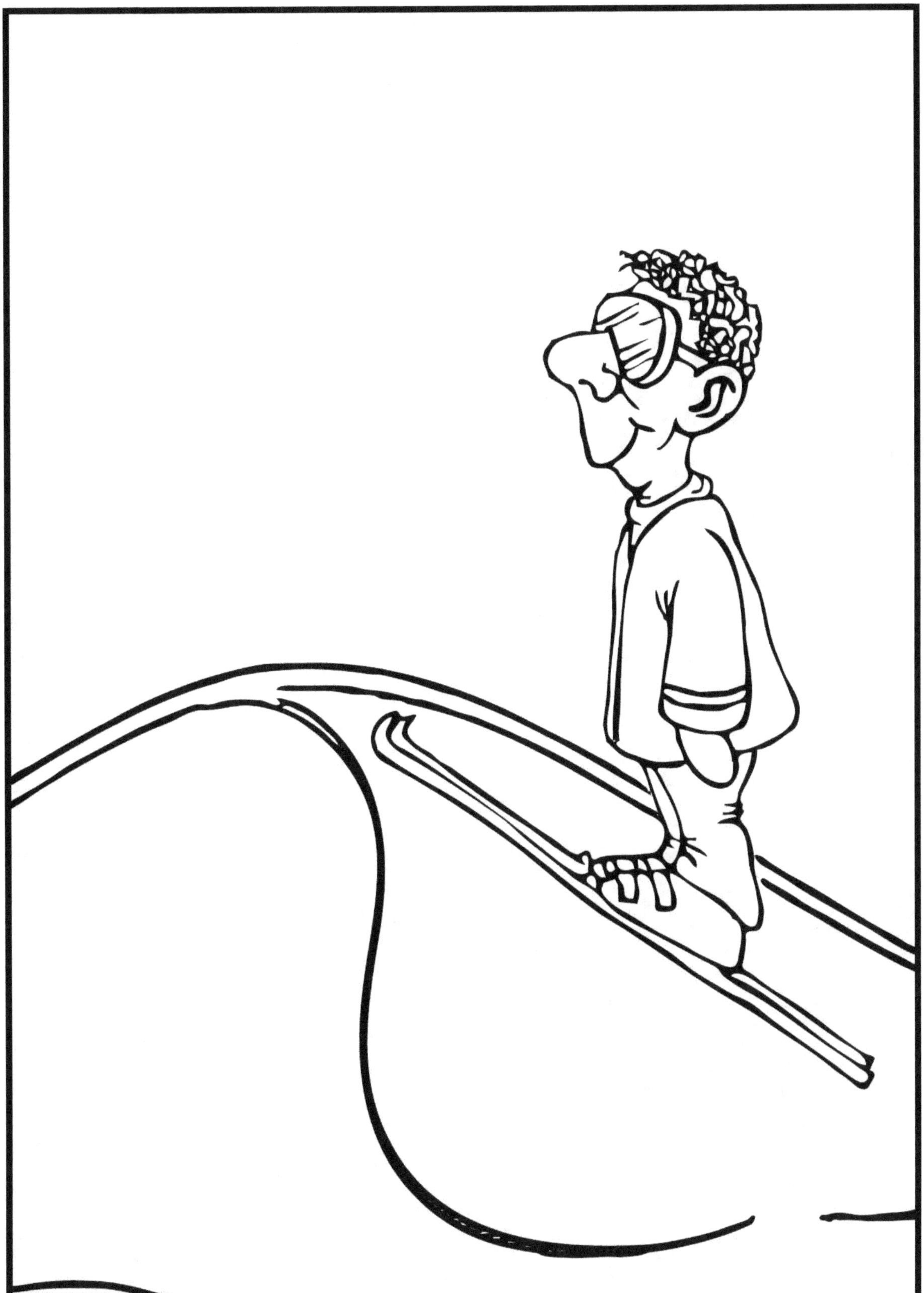

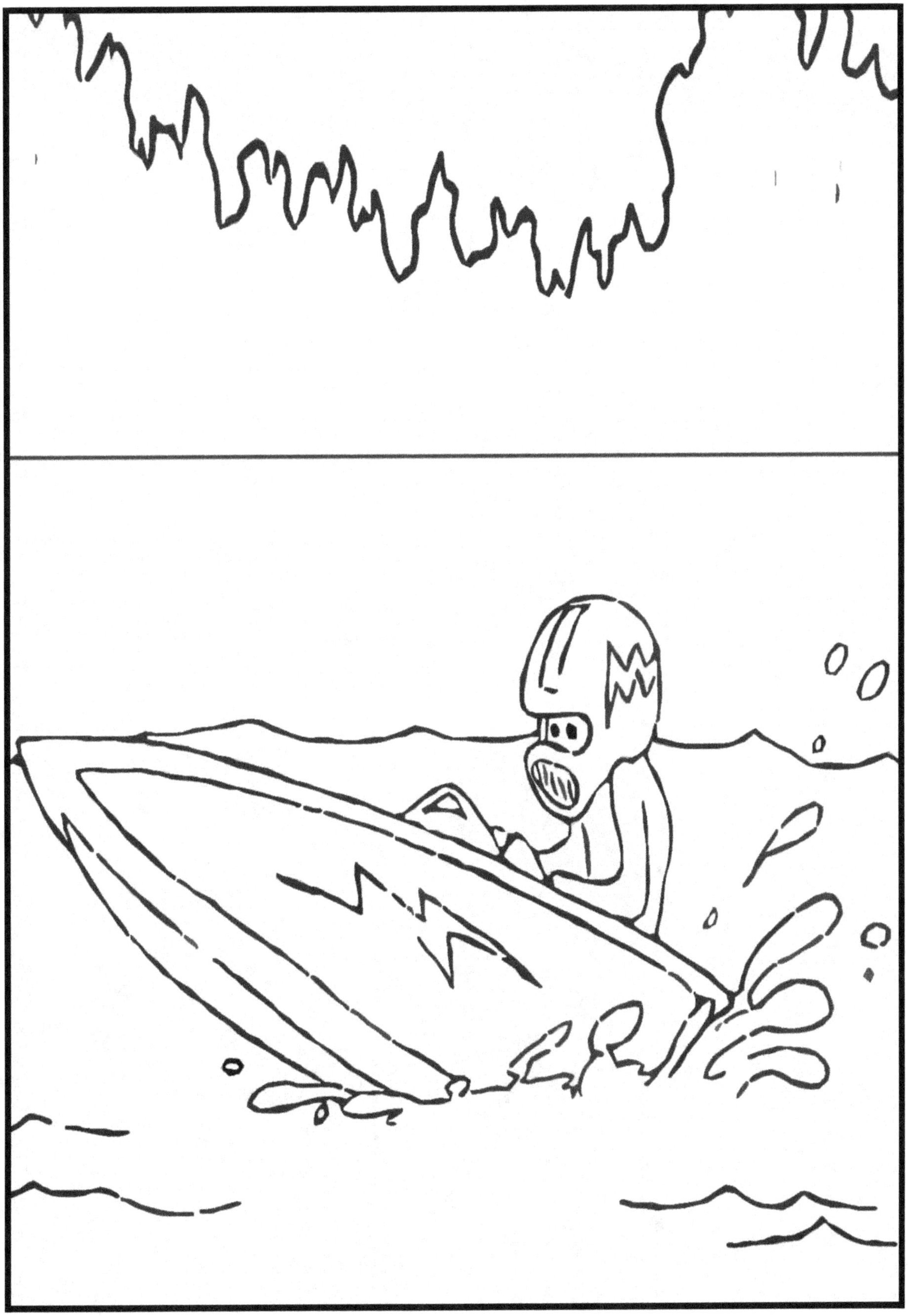

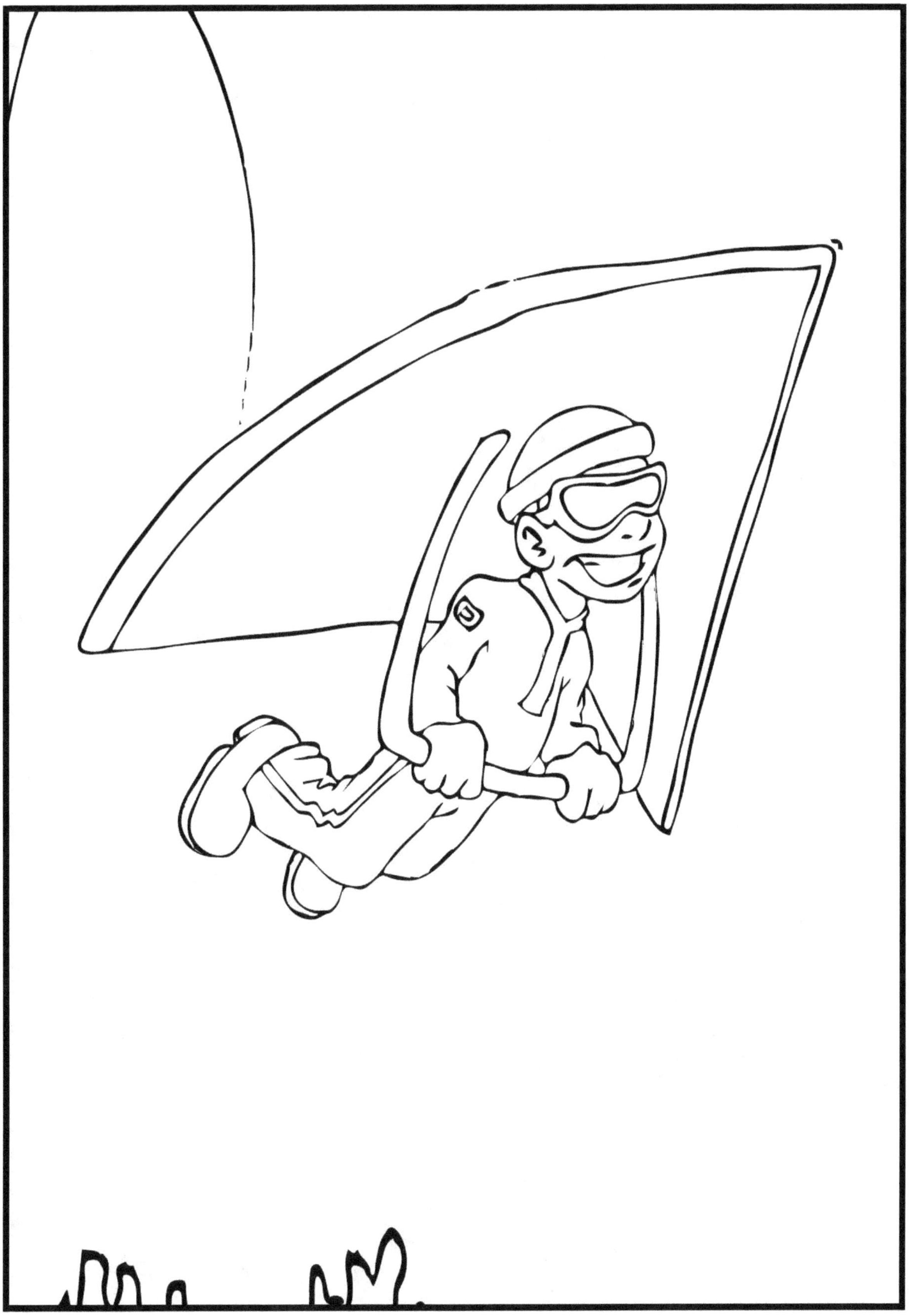

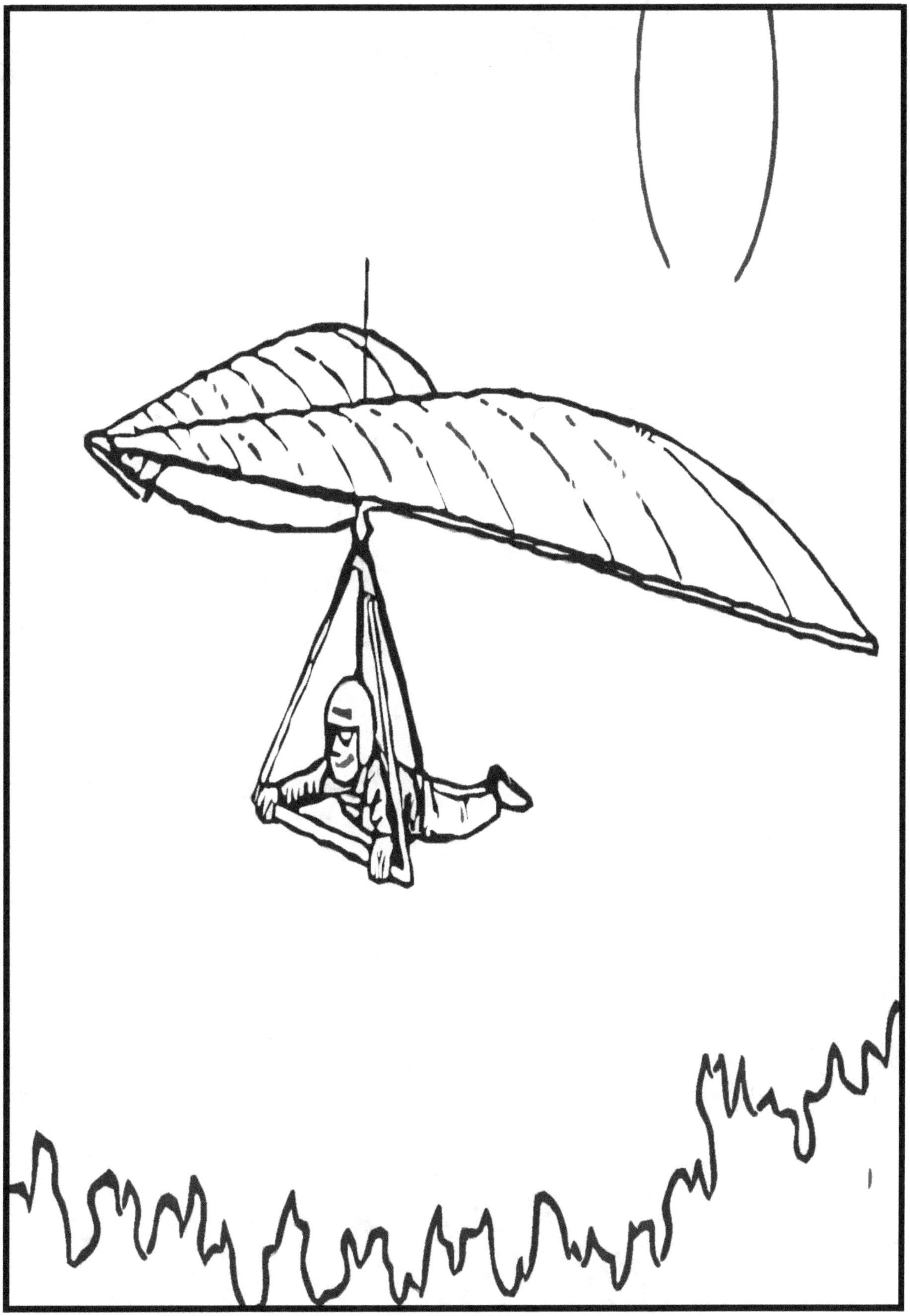

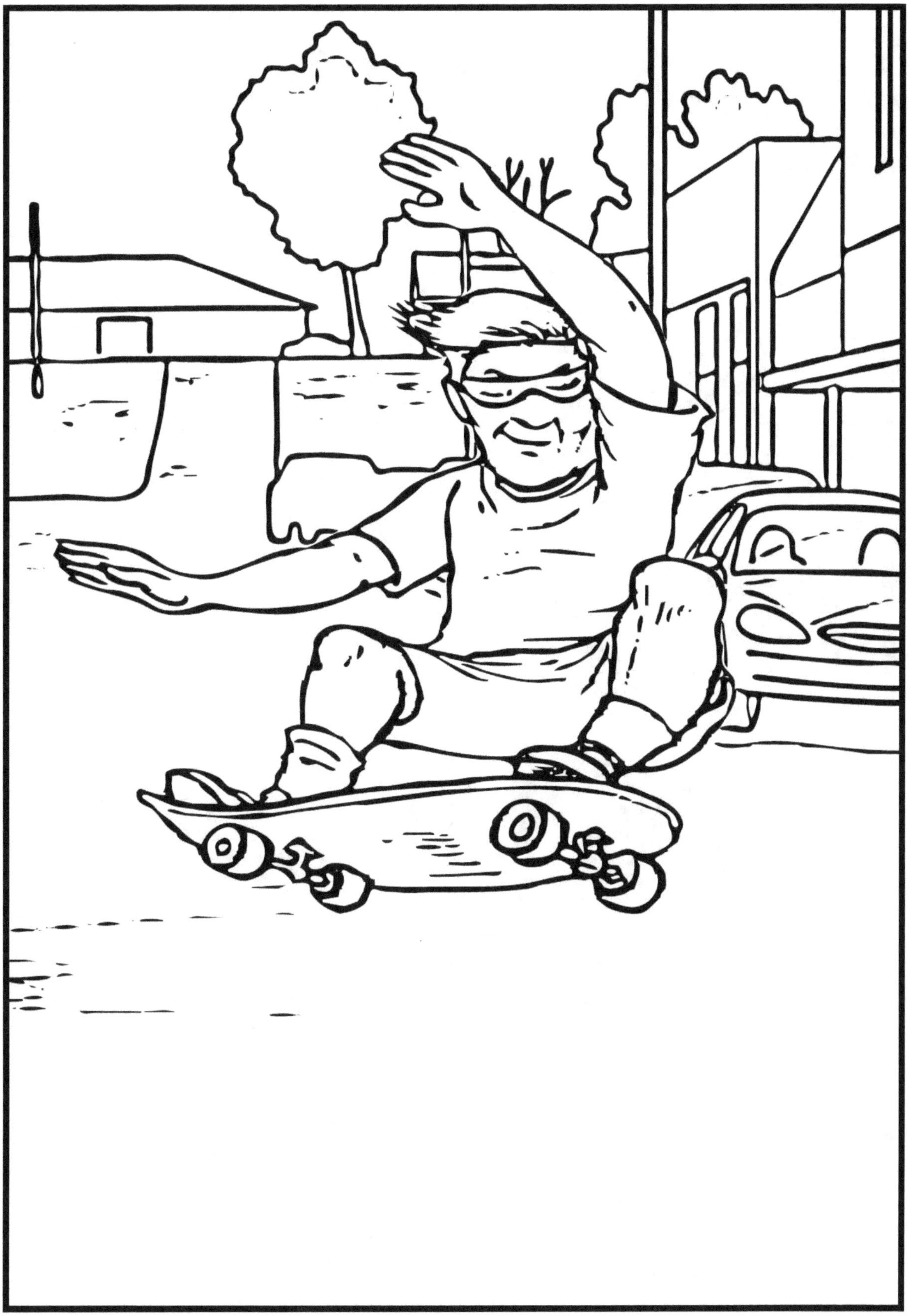

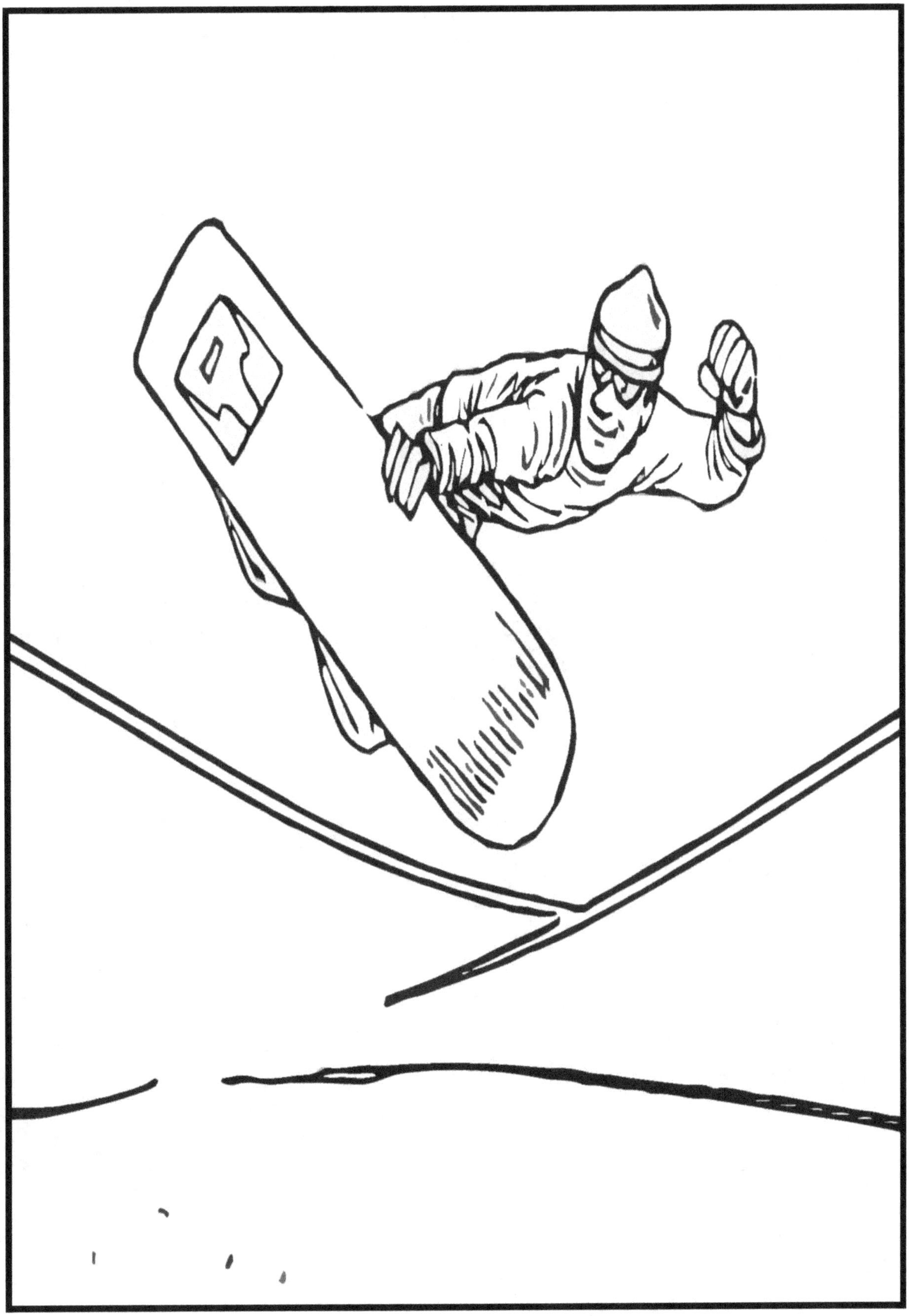

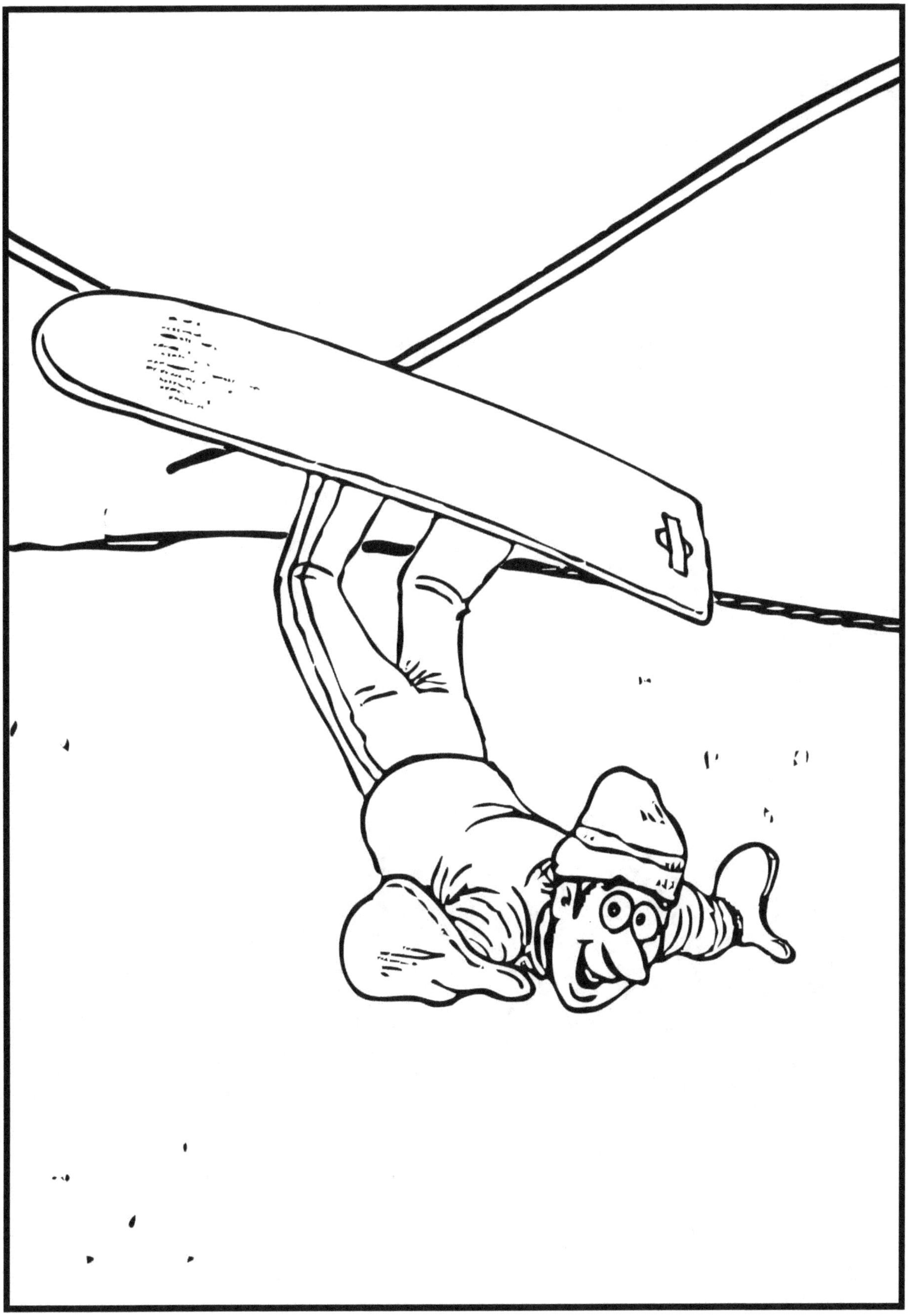

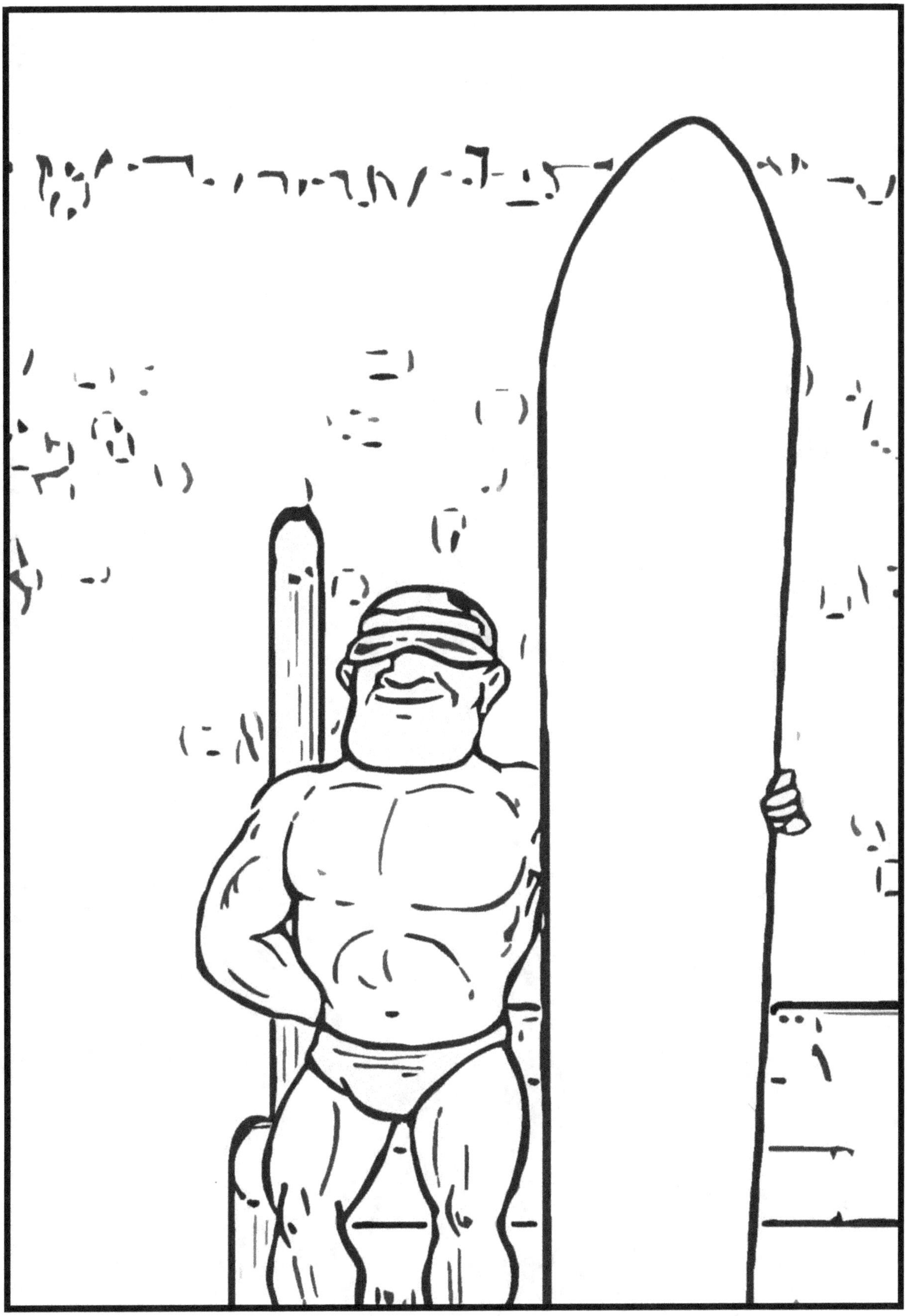

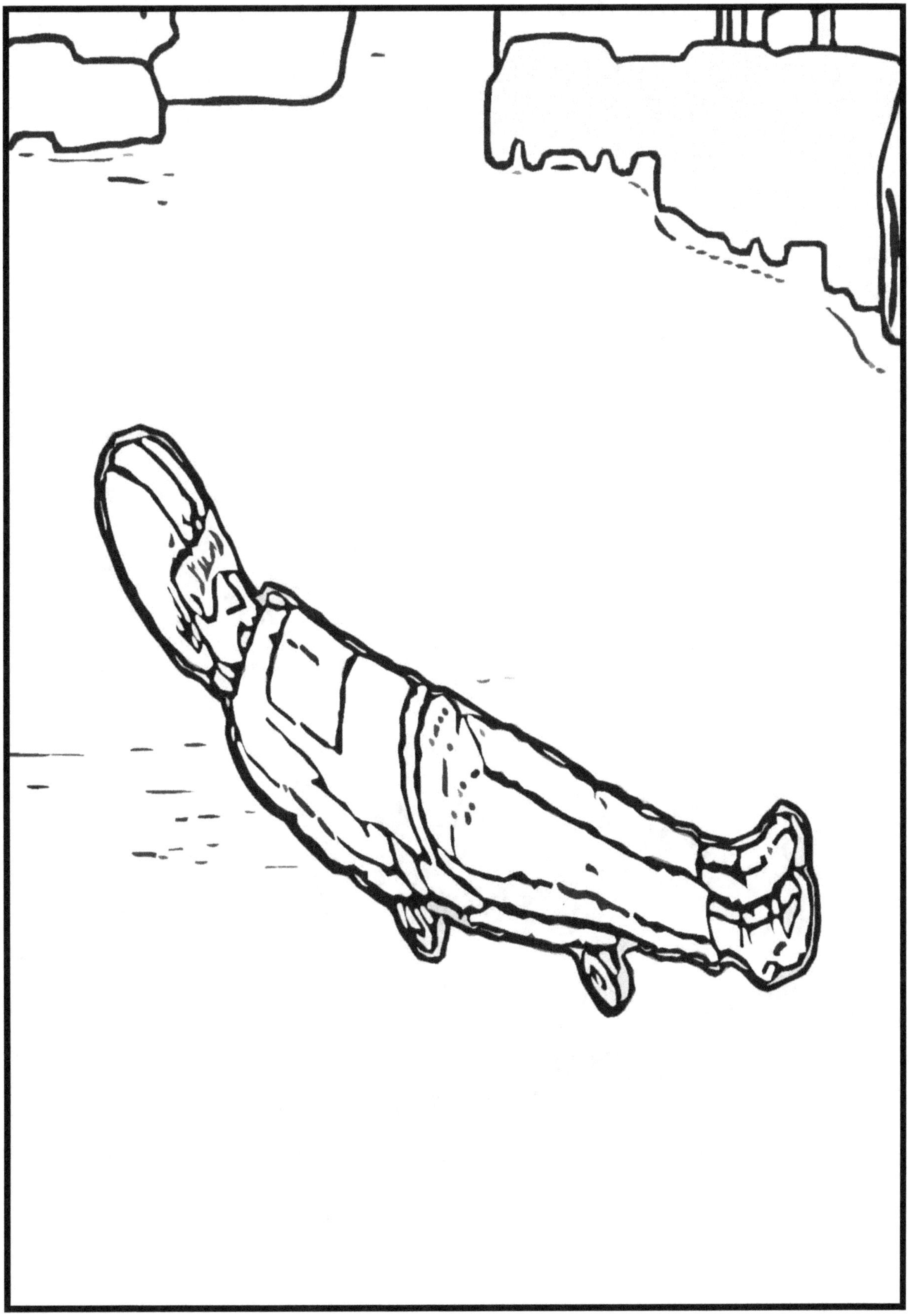

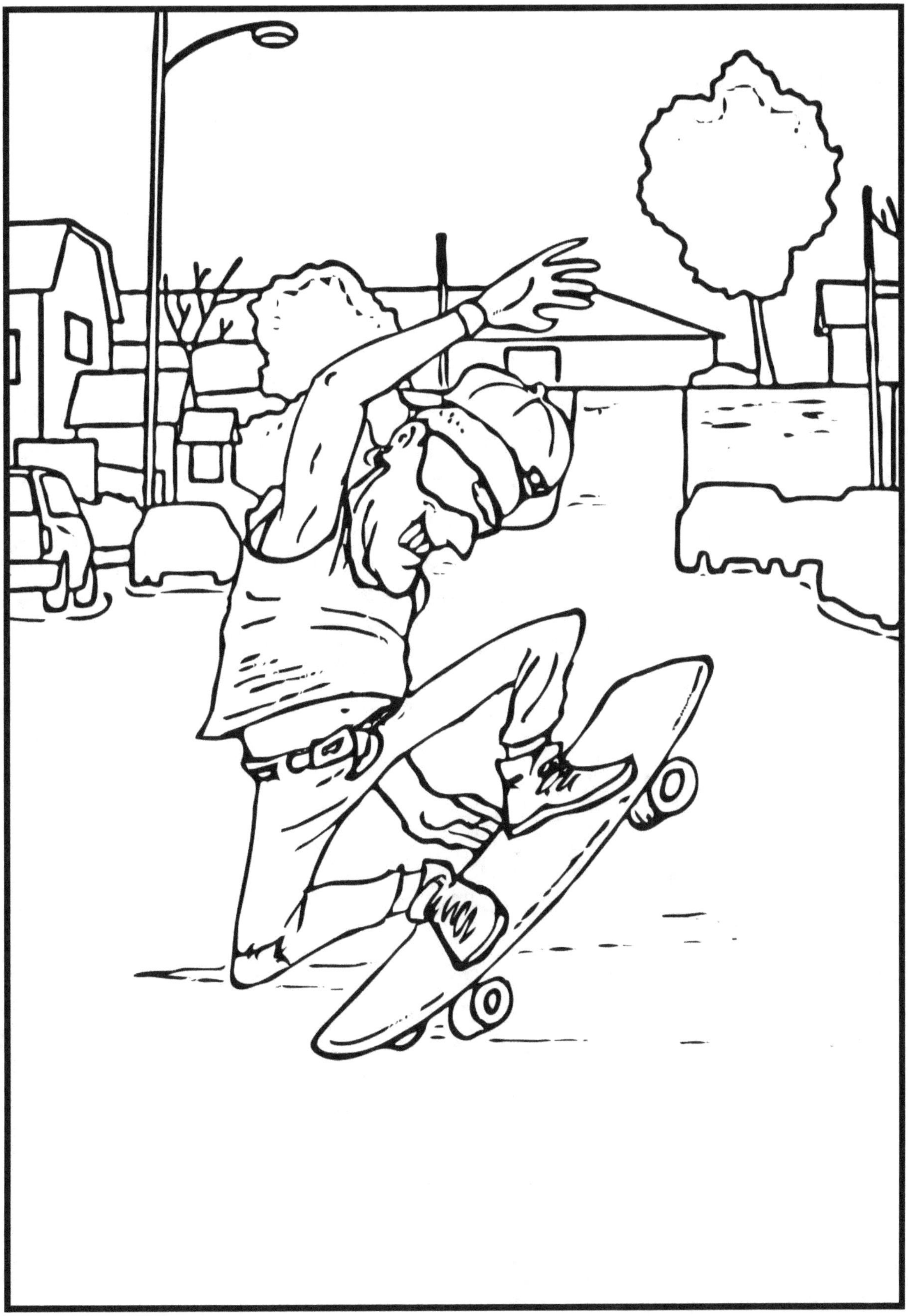

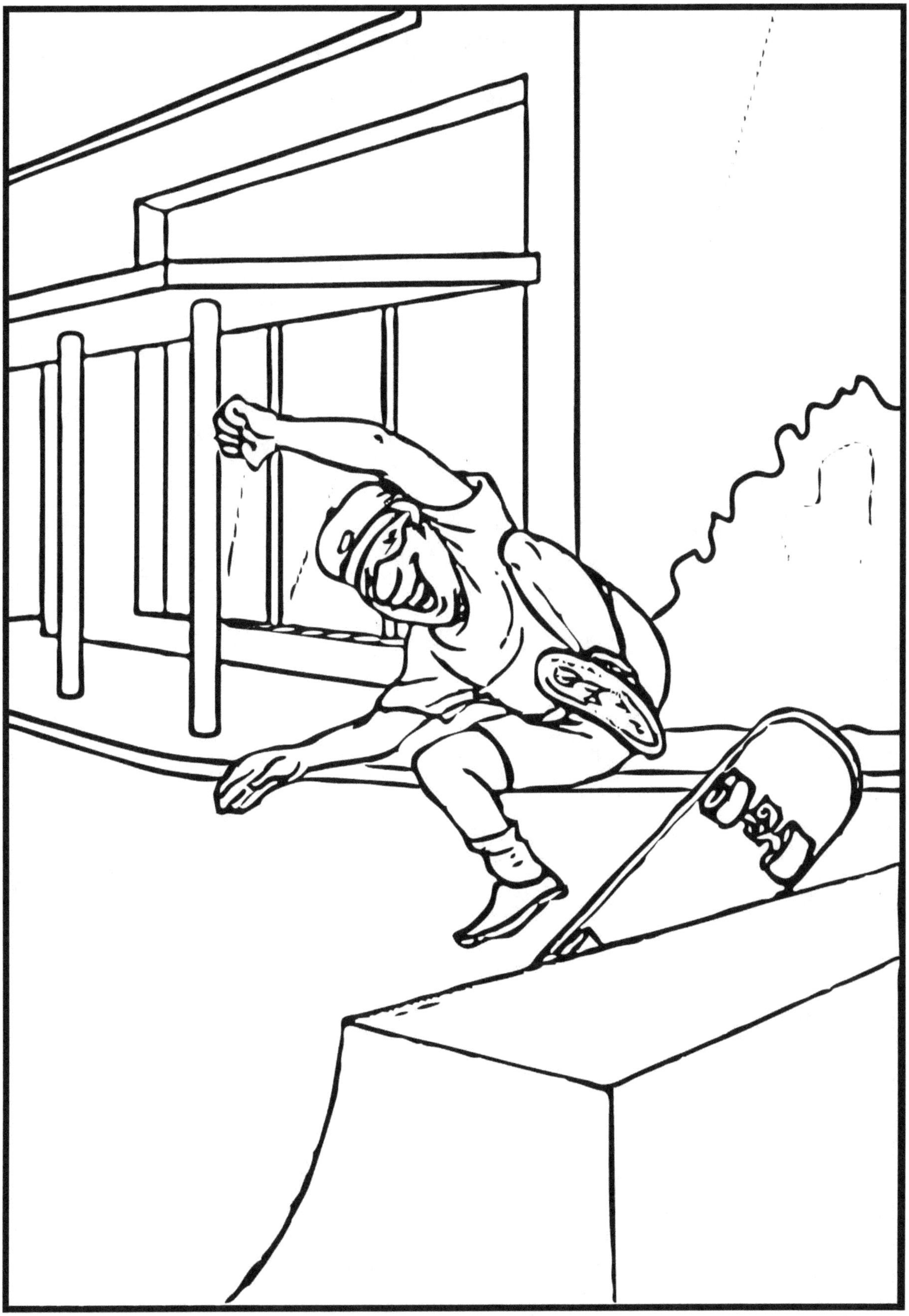

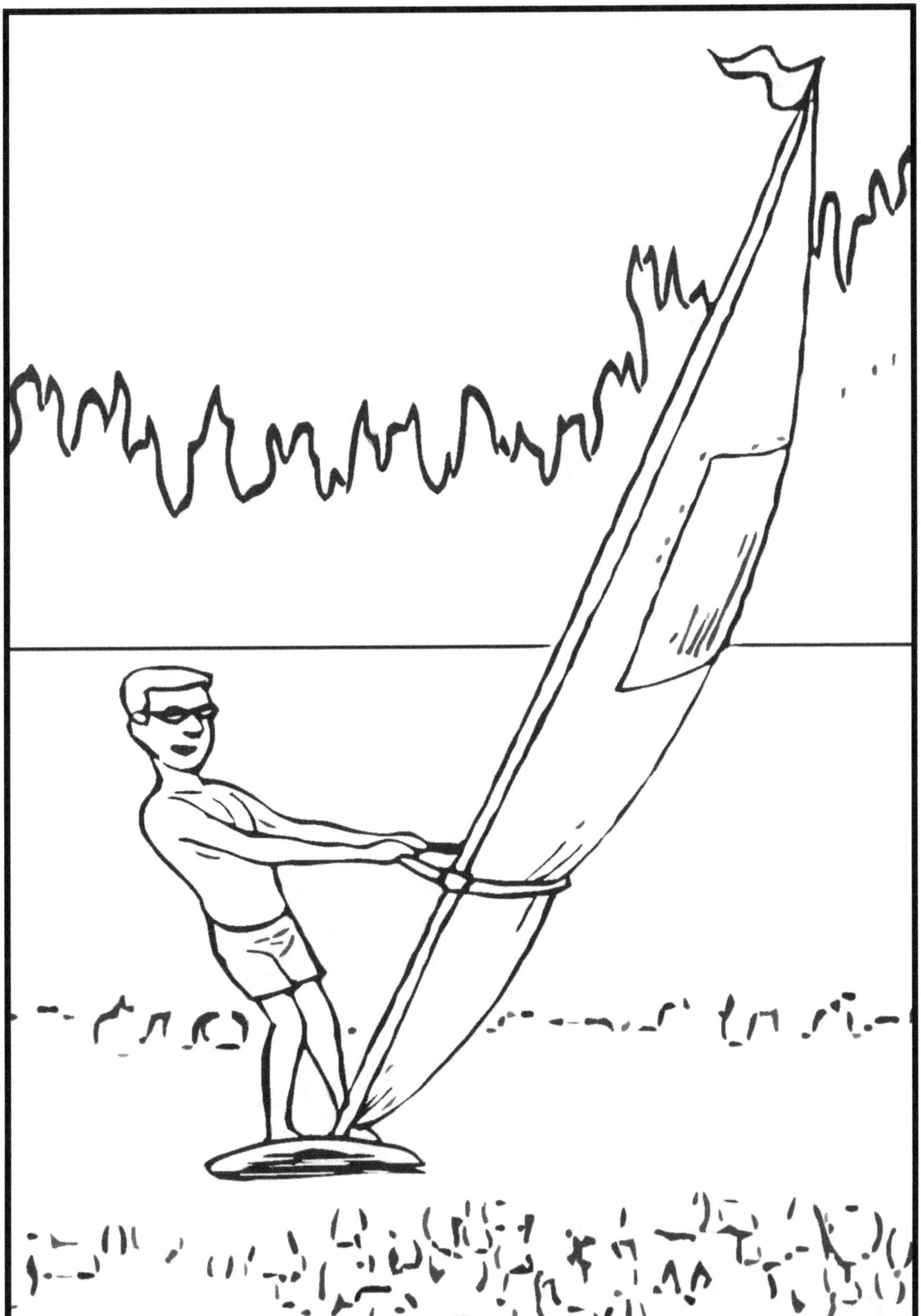

www.ingramcontent.com/pod-product-compliance
Lightning Source LLC
Chambersburg PA
CBHW081311180526
45170CB00007B/2661
* 9 7 8 1 5 2 2 9 0 2 1 5 7 *